Learning Laboratories
A Guide to Adoption and Use

LEARNING LABORATORIES
A GUIDE TO ADOPTION AND USE

William G. Teachey
and
Joseph B. Carter

Educational Technology Publications
Englewood Cliffs, New Jersey 07632

Printed in the United States of America.

Library of Congress Catalog Card Number: 75-125872.

International Standard Book Number:
0-87778-010-2.

First Printing.
Second Printing: August, 1972.

ABOUT THE AUTHORS

William G. Teachey, formerly Assistant Director, Britannica Center for Studies in Learning and Motivation, Hollins College, Roanoke, Virginia and Vice President, Behavioral Research Laboratories, Palo Alto, California, is President, Learning Lab Associates, Inc., and Learning Lab Arts and Publishers, Inc., Roanoke, Virginia.

Joseph B. Carter is Coordinator of Learning Laboratories, Department of Community Colleges, Raleigh, North Carolina.

CONTENTS

Learning Laboratories

A Guide to Adoption and Use

Introduction to Individualized
Instruction in the Learning Lab

CHAPTER ONE

INTRODUCTION TO INDIVIDUALIZED
INSTRUCTION IN THE LEARNING LAB

PROCEDURES AND METHODOLOGY

The learning laboratory can be defined as an accumulation of constructed programmed and self-instructional materials. These materials are arranged by subject in a logical sequence in relation to grade level and area of general interest. The instructional technique is dependent upon the methodology which follows:

1. As the teacher is the key person in most schools and college courses, the *coordinator* is the key person in the learning lab. The role of the traditional teacher must change when a new instructional technique is introduced. The coordinator serves as the facilitator in the learning process. The coordinator is trained in programmed and self-instructional techniques, and he is capable of making educational decisions and directing students through their assignments.

2. The coordinator interviews, counsels and seeks to establish rapport and to develop an effective line of communication with each student.

3. Each student is given a diagnostic inventory in reading and math. *An English test is also given if his reading level is sixth grade or above.* Deficiencies are noted and an individualized curriculum developed relative to the student's reading ability and stated objectives. Having evaluated the student by means of counseling and testing, appropriate programs are prescribed to take the student from where he is to where he wants to go. However, the choice of "electing" to take these courses is up to the student. If the student objects to prescribed courses, he is allowed to take the desired course. The door is always open for him to return to his real need.

4. The student is thoroughly introduced to programmed instruction. Most students, as a result of previous

learning experiences, have been conditioned to learn by reading, listening, interacting with teacher and students or a combination of these factors. The coordinator's main purpose here is to re-orient the student to individualized instruction. A working relationship between coordinator and student is established, whereby the student depends upon the program to teach him on a one-to-one ratio, but he is aware that he can receive necessary help from the coordinator.

5. Students are placed at a level at which they are likely to achieve success. They are challenged by the more difficult material, but are not bored by the remedial skills. The student sets his own best pace that will allow at least an 85 percent rate of comprehension. Frustration is reduced to a minimum.

6. Since there are no formal classes, a realistic schedule is established for each student. Each student is encouraged to attend four to six hours per week or a minimum of two hours per subject per week. If students spend less than the specified time, they do not feel the true sense of accomplishment which should be felt by all students. In addition to the established schedule, students are encouraged to work in the lab at any convenient time as often as they desire. This type of scheduling does not interfere with other responsibilities.

7. Chapter, unit and posttests are administered to make sure that the student obtains 85 percent or higher. If

maximum progress is not being made, program changes follow. If desired, each learning lab may also contain a series of standardized tests applicable to the most popular subjects.

ADVANTAGES

The learning laboratory has many advantages over the traditional classroom setting with respect to improved instruction and student attitudes toward the learning process. They are:

1. Every student in the lab achieves success, as a result of the nature of programmed instruction.

2. The instructional materials used in the labs reduce pupil frustration, since each student sets his own pace, based on his rate of comprehension.

3. Personality conflicts are significantly reduced, since the student interacts with the programmed text and coordinator, who is always present when the lab is open.

4. The labs are designed to meet individual needs on a variety of levels—educational, social and psychological.

5. Scheduling is flexible. For example, if due to inclement weather or illness the student misses his regularly scheduled period at the lab, he does not fall behind, as he would in a traditional classroom.

6. Beyond the materials which are supplied in all laboratories, students help select their own programs with respect to both curriculum and subject area, under the guidance of the coordinators.

7. The nature of the laboratory instructional materials compels the student to proceed forward in a logical manner, with minimum deviations from the program as it is outlined.

8. The mode of instruction in the laboratory is more comprehensive than traditional teaching, in addition to being subject to less bias.

9. The programs offered to the student in the laboratory have a greater continuity than their traditional counterparts, in that the same program may be picked up in another laboratory somewhere else in the state.

10. In general, the cost per student contact hour can be significantly reduced in the setting of a learning laboratory as compared with a traditional classroom.

The Role
of the Coordinator

CHAPTER TWO

THE ROLE OF THE COORDINATOR

The coordinator has a varied role to perform in a learning center, one which encompasses these positions:

1. Counselor
2. Test administrator
3. Tutor or teacher
4. Supervisor and bookkeeper
5. Curriculum specialist

On one level, the coordinator is the counterpart of the traditional teacher. In this capacity it is his responsibility to create a favorable climate for effective and meaningful student/subject matter interaction fundamental to the learning process designed to occur in the center. Ideally, the coordinator, in order to carry out this activity, should have a strong background in self-instructional learning techniques. In addition, he must be able to provide students with direction in their work and to make and implement decisions in the realm of education.

THE INITIAL INTERVIEW

Another aspect of the coordinator's job is to act in the capacity of an interviewer and a counselor, a person who attempts to establish rapport and to develop an open line of communication with each student who comes to the center.

The initial interview is designed to help the coordinator establish rapport with a potential student. At this time, the coordinator should:

1.   Learn what the applicant desires. Ask such questions as:
   a.   What is your goal?
   b.   Why did you come?
   c.   When will you be able to come to the center?
   The answers to these and similar questions may

affect the actual placement of a student into a program.

2. Discuss the student's needs as he (the student) defines them.

3. Indirectly encourage the student to make a verbal statement of the objectives which he hopes to realize at the center. This statement should become the basis for increasing levels of student motivation.

4. Request that the student fill out an application form.

5. Check over the completed form with the student.

If another prospective student is waiting, the coordinator should give him an application form to complete and some descriptive information about the center (e.g., "The Learning Laboratory Presents: A New Way to Learn").

STUDENT'S INTRODUCTION TO
SELF-INSTRUCTION

The coordinator should then explain to the student how the laboratory operates and what that student can expect to achieve with respect to the goals which he has outlined. It has been demonstrated that the success of the student is enhanced if the coordinator follows this procedure in introducing the student to programmed and other self-instructional techniques:

1. Look through several programs related to the pupil's objectives with the student.

2. Show and explain the process of learning on a one-to-one basis by showing sample frames and explaining that each such unit of instruction contains an important bit of information to be learned and that the frames increase in both difficulty and complexity as one proceeds further into a program.

3. Permit the student to answer frames in order for the materials to win him over to programmed instruction as a valid learning device.

4. Take the student on a tour of the lab, showing him where the various materials are stored.

5. Tell the student, and be sincere and show concern when you say it, that his interest, patience and determination will be the major factors in his success and in the eventual realization of his goals.

At this time, the placement testing should begin. In light of the fears which many persons hold concerning testing, the coordinator should emphasize that the tests are administered solely for placement purposes—and that there is no passing or failing grade. It is highly recommended that tests be referred to as "placement inventories" until the student conquers his fears about testing.

While the student is engaged in taking his first placement test, the coordinator should make out a time card on the student based on the information provided on the application and a file folder.

Areas of deficiency indicated by the tests are noted by the coordinator; and, on the basis of these, an individualized curriculum designed to erase those gaps is developed so that the student may begin to move toward the realization of his goals. The student may override the coordinator in the selection of programs of study, but he naturally has the option to go back later and make up these previously recognized deficiencies in his background. For example, if a student is insistent on beginning algebra despite the fact he is not reading on a ninth grade level, he may do so. Yet, at the same time, he is encouraged to improve his reading skills so that he will be able to comprehend the material presented in the programs in algebra.

The students must be placed at a level on which they are able to achieve immediate success and still be challenged. From there, the student proceeds upward and onward at a rate of speed which allows maximum comprehension (at least 85 percent). This type of placement, in addition to the role which it plays in the reduction of frustration, is designed to keep the student within the framework of the program and to maintain maximum motivation and learning.

The student and the coordinator should work together in establishing a tentative schedule of work in the center for the pupil. In order that the student may develop a sense of accomplishment in his work, it is suggested that the minimum time spent at the center per week be four to six hours or two hours per subject. No maximum amount of time is set on student participation in the lab, since "extra" time spent in the center helps the student to move toward the realization of his goals more quickly and provides increased doses of reinforcement fundamental to learning.

As a test administrator, the coordinator is concerned not only with placement inventories, but also with a variety of other tests—pre, chapter, unit, and post (final and standardized). These are administered at appropriate points to insure that the student is working at a minimum level of 85 percent comprehension. If the student is not performing at this level, appropriate changes in a given student's curriculum are in order.

Thus far, the coordinator has emerged as a person who is initially concerned with test administration, teaching in the sense of planning appropriate courses of study for each student, tutoring in the sense of placing the student in alternative programs or having him review certain areas of a given program, and counseling. Of the roles discussed thus far, the last—counseling—is the most pervasive by far.

The student must know that you are interested in him as an individual. Ultimately, however, you will be more valuable to him as a resource person if you show him *the way to the answers he seeks* instead of telling him what they are. A suggested procedure is:

1. Be sure you understand the student's questions.
2. Utilize an inductive approach.
3. Permit the student to show that he has reached an understanding.
4. If necessary, give the student additional practice or review exercises.

If you find that you are unable to assist the student in arriving at a solution to the riddle(s) which he has encountered, try to find out the necessary information from a colleague. If the student, and ultimately the center itself, is to succeed, personnel must act as a team.

The coordinator's role in the learning lab is broader yet. He is also a bookkeeper and a supervisor for the lab. In the latter capacity he works to:

1. Promote the lab.
2. Recruit students.
3. Order and reorder materials.
4. Maintain a pleasant physical atmosphere.

As in most bookkeeping roles, the coordinator's responsibilities in the area require the completion of a wide variety of forms.

Before you begin your responsibilities at the center, consider the following suggestions which were made by your colleagues on the basis of their experience:

1. Read through as many programs as you can so that you can meet the needs of the student more effectively.

2. Study along with the students if you have any free time. They will not feel that they are alone in their need to improve if you do this.

3. Be flexible.

4. Be friendly with your students. A smile or a kind word when they arrive and depart will make them feel good and will make the center an attractive place to work in their eyes, especially on the very important first day.

5. Do not be afraid to praise a student for good work. Everyone likes recognition.

6. Be a good listener; let the students confide in you.

7. Develop a philosophy of care and concern.

8. Treat all students as *individuals.*

9. Be honest and sincere with your students at all

times. You cannot fool them!

10. Do your best with each student. If you do this, do not concern yourself too much with dropouts from the center. Many people are simply "drop-ins" who come to see what is going on and who lack dedication and initiative to improve.

SUMMARY

1. *Counselor*

The learning lab coordinator must establish rapport with each student. An open line of communication must be developed and maintained during the entire course of study. The initial interview is important in that the student must feel that he has been accepted and that there is a sincere desire for the coordinator to help him. Allow time for the student to verbally state his objective. The counseling must be directive in encouraging the student to state his need for academic as well as vocational advancement. A good point to remember: work with each student on a personal basis. Help the student to develop a sense of accomplishment initially in order to sustain motivation.

2. *Test Administrator*

Testing is a vital phase of the learning lab coordinator's responsibility. He or she should become familiar with all types of tests used in the lab, as well as the purpose and need of such tests. A competent test administrator will use test results in helping the student. In analyzing results, use such phrases as: "you need a review in this area." Refrain from stating specific grade levels.

3. *Tutor or Teacher*

Since the learning lab employs a new instructional concept, the role of the traditional teacher must change to guarantee maximum effectiveness of the lab as an instructional system. The instruction is individualized through the use of programmed and self-instructional materials. The coordinator must establish a working relationship with each student so that he will depend upon the program to teach him on a one-to-one ratio—but the student is also aware that he can receive the necessary help when and if he needs assistance. The coordinator is no longer the primary giver of information, but acts as the catalyst or facilitator in the learning process. He brings the student and materials together, provides for a meaningful learning experience, and rewards and encourages each student. The amount of assistance given to students will vary with each student. Some students need more help than others, but always remember that your role as a coordinator is not that of a teacher—your assistance is terminated after you have helped the student over the hurdle or "rough spot."

4. *Supervisor and Bookkeeper*

The lab does not operate on a short block or class schedule. Students are free to come and go; however, a realistic schedule should be developed for each student. This mode of operation demands greater control and more accurate procedures for record keeping. The coordinator should be in complete charge of the lab and present when the lab is open. The lab should not be left open for students to use without adequate supervision. Any change in administration, techniques, procedures, and operation should be approved by the coordinator. He or she should have the authority to maintain control and provide for a quiet and stimulating environment for learning.

The coordinator also serves as a bookkeeper in maintaining accurate and adequate reports on each student. However, the time card can be best utilized in keeping an accurate number of hours that each student has spent in the lab. The use and method of completion must be fully explained to each student. Each student must develop independence in helping himself in the lab. He must be taught how to complete the time card, and he must be checked to make sure that it is completed at the beginning and end of each period of instruction. The date must be recorded, the time started, the time finished and total hours, recorded to nearest half-hour. The last frame completed should also be recorded in the space provided. One time card should be kept for each subject taken.

5. *Curriculum Specialist*

The coordinator has the responsibility of constructing a tailored curriculum for each student. A program is developed for the student, rather than fitting the student into a curriculum. The factors considered in developing the curriculum include: (1) frustration level in reading, math and English; (2) areas of interest, such as hobbies, likes and dislikes; (3) personal economic and social conditions; and (4) vocational interests.

Reading is the core subject, and placement into other

subjects is dependent upon the reading level. The whole concept of the learning lab is that the student is never asked to do something that he is not capable of doing.

The reading curriculum must be established first, unless the student is reading at a level equal to or higher than that required by the student goal or objective.

It is not uncommon for program changes to be made during the student's course of study. The student should become familiar with all reading materials and gradually develop independence in selecting those materials best suited for his particular need. The student should be encouraged to spend at least two hours per week per subject.

The Math Placement Inventory Chart is less difficult to interpret because of direct placement into a program. In placing a student into a math program, keep in mind his reading level. A good rule of thumb is to place a student in a subject area that is written at least one grade level below the student's reading level. Math program changes can also be made to accommodate individual needs. The Math Inventory can be used as a diagnostic test in determining those areas in which the student needs help. Example: A student may have difficulty solving long division problems, but has mastered the skill of adding fractions. The student is placed in long division, and is allowed to skip the concepts in which he has no difficulty.

The development of curricula in English, social studies, and science are conducted in a similar manner.

Physical Facilities

CHAPTER THREE

PHYSICAL FACILITIES

The facilities that exist in various learning labs will vary; however, the basic requirements include such items as coordinator's desk, tables, chairs, student sign-in cabinet, file cabinets, shelving, carrels, and a room large enough to adequately accommodate some 20 students. The coordinator's desk should be near the door in a position to observe all students.

Tables and carrels are used for work areas. Both are used, since it is learned that some students prefer to work at a table with other students and some prefer to work more independently at their carrel or booth. Generally, when a student selects his own work area, he will maintain the same area on returning for additional sessions.

Typical school desks, it should be noted, have been found to be both inadequate and inappropriate.

INSTALLATION REQUIREMENTS

Learning Lab Room

1. *Size*—to accommodate 20 enrollees, the minimum room size is 600 square feet.
2. *Lighting*—shall be diffused fluorescent, preferably in accordance with Illuminating Engineering Society standards for schools.
3. *Heating and Cooling*—shall be controlled so that the temperature range is between 70 and 80 degrees and the humidity between 35 and 45 percent.
4. *Noise Level*—shall be controlled by installing sound-baffling material between carrels and/or installing ceiling and wall-mounted sound-baffling material in work table areas.

5. *Rest Room Facilities*—shall be provided for both boys and girls (or men and women in adult centers).

Furniture and Facilities

1. *Coordinator's Station*—includes:
   a. desk
   b. four-drawer file cabinet, containing a permanent file for each enrollee and master files of inventories
   c. enrollee Time Card File
2. *Enrollees' Work Station*—shall include both tables and carrels, since some enrollees prefer to work independently at a carrel or booth and some prefer to work at a table with others. Desks should not be used. The work stations shall be arranged in such a way as to ease the traffic flow, since enrollees may be entering and leaving at different times. Work stations shall be provided for 20 students.
3. *Learning Materials Storage*—shall include a minimum of 220 linear feet of shelving. Since most enrollees are working on reading, the reading materials should be displayed on a large table near

the center of the room or in a position accessible to most enrollees. This will only be possible if the room exceeds the minimum size requirements.

LOCATION OF THE LEARNING LAB

The lab should be readily accessible to the enrollees. An excellent potential physical location for the learning lab would be the school, college or technical library. In this learning environment a qualified librarian would function as the coordinator. As a matter of fact, some of the most successful learning labs have been operated in support of the total service offered by the library for learning resource centers.

Testing

CHAPTER FOUR

TESTING

THEORY AND METHODOLOGY

Testing, however controversial, is fundamental to the success of any instructional program. On one level, its importance may be demonstrated by the fact that test questions provide immediate reinforcement for high marks, particularly in an individualized instructional situation. On another level, testing programs serve to help the instructor assess the student's achievements academically.

The assessment of the student in the laboratory begins the moment the prospective student and the coordinator meet for the first time. The procedure for carrying out an initial assessment should include the following:

1. Establish rapport with the student.

2. Encourage the student to make a verbal assessment of his objective.

3. Administer a placement inventory or a series of placement inventories. At this time, it is extremely important that the coordinator does not use the words "test" or "examination" with the student, since the student may fear psychological measurements.

Regardless of the number of tests a student has taken previously, pretesting by the coordinator is necessary, except where local institutions have utilized the *same placement tests* as the center and these scores are available.

Persons who serve as test administrators should be well acquainted with both the general value and psychological bases of testing. More specifically, they should familiarize themselves with the following terminology:

1. *Percentile*. This is the point below which a certain number of scores in a distribution fall. The 62nd percentile, for instance, tells one that 62 percent of the total number of scores were either at that point

or below.

2. *Validity*. A given test ought to perform the function for which it was developed. An achievement test, for example, should measure the student's knowledge in all areas of material presented in a given curriculum, while aptitude or placement tests should serve as a predictive measure of future success in a given area of study.

3. *Reliability*. In order to be reliable, the test should measure the same skill acquisitions each time it is given to the same person.

NOTE: No test is 100 percent valid or reliable.

4. *Mode*. This is the score which most people made. It is, in short, the most fashionable score for a group.

5. *Median*. A median score is the middle score indicating that 50 percent of a group scored above that point and 50 percent below.

6. *Mean*. Often called the arithmetic mean, this score is the average score, the total of all scores made by a group and then divided by the number of persons in that group.

7. *Average*. Measure of central tendency—mean, median, and mode, for example—are frequently referred to in this manner.

The student must be properly introduced to the nature

of testing if he is to remain in the center and begin work which will carry him toward the realization of his objectives. Consequently, it is suggested that you convey the nature of the testing program to the student in this way:

1. Inform the student that you are there to help him.

2. Explain to him that programmed instruction is a new method or way of learning which is far more effective than traditional classroom instruction. Tell him about the advantages of the lab over a regular classroom as they relate to his previous and current educational experiences.

3. Indicate to him that learning in this situation will be more meaningful to him now than in previous educational environments.

4. Tell him he will need to take a placement inventory or check to determine which program(s) of study will be best suited to his needs and interests.

5. Inform him that this is *not* a test he can pass or fail.

6. Explain to the student the following facts about the tests:

    a. No one is expected to complete all items.

    b. Items increase in difficulty.

    c. When an item is too difficult, do not guess.

7. Request that the student return the inventory booklet and answer sheet to you when he is finished.

It is strongly suggested that you complete the following procedures with the student before administering the placement inventory:

1. Ask him if he is familiar with multiple-choice questions.

2. Let him work through sample questions at your desk.

3. Make sure the student understands that he is to write on the separate answer sheet (if provided), not in the test booklet.

4. Check the student's answers on sample questions.

5. Indicate to the student that there is no time limit.

If two students are taking the same inventory, seat them at different tables or in individual study carrels.

TYPES OF TESTING

Four types of testing are utilized in the learning lab or in association with it. They are:

1. Placement inventories or checks

2. Pretests for specific courses of study

3.   Chapter and/or unit tests
4.   Posttest—final

PLACEMENT INVENTORIES AND INITIAL PLACEMENT

Testing is your best tool for placing the student in the most beneficial course, but it takes practice to skillfully read and evaluate a placement inventory. It is not a cut-and-dried, right-or-wrong situation. Several forms of placement inventories are administered in the labs and cover these areas:

1.   Reading
2.   Mathematics

1. *Reading.* A reading inventory is given to all students who enter the lab. The coordinator should be able, however, to predict fairly accurately the student's reading level from information gained in the initial interview—such as favorite hobbies and the amount and type of reading which a pupil has done.

The Reading Placement Inventory is administered at the end of the initial counseling session. It is most desirable that the tests be administered on an individual basis. However, group testing may be conducted if the students have been properly counseled and are informed as to what will be expected of them.

The Reading Placement Inventory is scored for each student. Care should be taken to observe the time it took each student to complete the tests, the number of correct items, and total items left blank. This will give you more information concerning the behavior of the student.

There are two methods of obtaining a starting level, since the test is designed to determine the frustration level in reading: (1) A student may be placed at the first grade level in which 50 percent or more of the items are missed. (2) A student may be placed at that point in which two consecutive items are missed.

Since no test is 100 percent valid and since the degree of validity varies from one test to another, adjustments may have to be made after initial placement by the coordinator to ensure that the pupil is on step. ("On step" is simply that level at which the student is challenged by increasingly complex material, further motivated by his successes to achieve greater heights, and freed from the boredom accompanying work which is remedial in nature.) In short, the student should be maintained in a state of intellectual arousal at all times during his educational experience at the center.

Frequent inspection checks are highly recommended during the first hours a student is working with the materials, in order to determine if he is responding favorably to both self-instructional techniques and to a given program of study. If this is not the case, a change of program is in order.

Reading skills and the ability to utilize them are

fundamental to success and achievement in other areas of study. When you consider placement into a subject other than reading, think reading first. Additionally, it is highly recommended that the student be placed down one grade level in other subjects from his reading level in order to increase the likelihood of success and to assure greater comprehension of the materials presented in a program of study.

2. *Mathematics.* The Math Placement Inventory, unlike the reading placement, is not administered to all students. The following persons should be given the test: (1) persons planning to take math courses, and (2) students preparing for an adult high school diploma or a high school equivalency certificate. Additionally, the student who is not yet reading at a fifth grade level should not take this inventory until he has worked successfully with reading materials for several study sessions. Placement in all subject areas is dependent on reading level.

If at all possible, the coordinator should not place a student in mathematics until the pupil is reading on at least a third grade level. Placement below this level of attainment in reading is advisable only if the coordinator feels that it is necessary to alleviate the boredom of the slow reading student.

Students are placed in programs of mathematics in

relation to their reading level and the results on the inventory.

As with a course of study in reading, the student should be placed and kept on step in his work and develop a pace whereby his rate of comprehension is at least 85 percent on all tests. If this level is not attained, the coordinator will analyze the errors and request the student to review that portion or portions of the program. In some instances, the coordinator may feel that another, yet comparable, program will meet a given student's needs more efficiently and effectively. When such a program change is made, the student should begin at that point where he demonstrated a weakness on a test.

Additionally, the coordinator should develop a close familiarity with the teacher's manual and, if applicable, additional supplements to programs. If he is familiar with the materials, the coordinator will know, for example, when he should supply such items as rulers, protractors, and compasses to the student.

If a student's raw score indicates that he should be placed, for example, in *English 2600,* you should start him in the unit which corresponds to the first skill area on the inventory in which the student answered 50 percent or more of the items incorrectly.

PRETESTS FOR INDIVIDUAL PROGRAMS

This phase of the testing program in the lab is far more circumscribed than any of the others. Frequently, such tests are not available. If they are, they should be administered to the student, particularly if he has already had the course under consideration elsewhere. The student's score and the coordinator's analysis of the questions which were missed will point up those areas in which the student needs review work. Thus, he will probably not have to go through the entire program.

CHAPTER AND/OR UNIT TESTS

These tests generally accompany programs. When no test is available, the coordinator would construct one which covers the materials covered in a given chapter or unit. *Note:* The words, "See coordinator for test exercise," should be stamped in red at the end of each chapter or unit.

If a student does not achieve a level of 85 percent comprehension, the coordinator may do several things in isolation or in combination. The possibilities are:

1.   Ask the student to correct his errors on the test. Go over the corrections with him.

2. Assign review units or chapters based on the material which the student missed. Write down both the page and the inclusive frame numbers so that the pupil may find the material more easily.

3. Administer an alternate form of the test—e.g., a pretest—when the student is cognizant of the errors that he made on the original test and if the student needs to further demonstrate his knowledge or to practice the test exercises.

POSTTESTS—FINAL AND STANDARDIZED

Final tests, which are administered when a student has completed a program, generally accompany most programs. They should always be the final exercise for each and every subject.

OPERATIONAL PROCEDURES IN TESTING

1. *Enrollee's Initial Reception*
   a. When an enrollee enters the lab for the first time, the coordinator interviews the enrollee to determine his educational objectives.

b. The coordinator will explain the lab to the new enrollee, demonstrating the kind of materials with which he will be working, by giving the enrollee a Demonstration Program, and working through it with him.

2. *Reading Assessment*

A Reading Placement Inventory is given to the new enrollee by the coordinator, and the results are entered on the enrollee's Test Record Card, to be kept in the enrollee's permanent file.

3. *Math and English Language Assessment*

Math and English Language Placement Inventories are given to the enrollee by the coordinator, and the results entered on the enrollee's Test Record Card. The appropriate Placement Charts are used by the coordinator to determine the specific programs and books to be begun by the enrollee in math and English. The coordinator assists the enrollee in filling out a Time Card for each of his first assignments in these subjects, and starts the enrollee on a reading, math, or English grammar assignment, according to the enrollee's preference.

4. *Placement in other learning materials*

The coordinator may also place the enrollee in social studies, science or available pre-vocational learning materials, depending upon the enrollee's educational objectives, as determined during the initial interview. A Time Card will be started for each such placement.

RECORD KEEPING

1. Permanent File for each enrollee—This file will be kept, in alphabetical order, by name, in the coordinator's file cabinet. It will contain completed Time Cards, the Learning Lab Application, the Curriculum Counseling Guide, Progression Charts for each subject the enrollee works on, and the Test Record Card. It is the responsibility of the coordinator to keep each enrollee's Permanent File up-to-date and complete.

2. Time Cards

    a. A Time Card is provided for each enrollee, for each programmed book. It contains the enrollee's name, name of material being used, date and time of beginning the material, and date and time of each period of use of the material.

    b. The coordinator will explain the use of the

Card when the enrollee first enters the lab, and will daily supervise the enrollee as he fills out the Card.

c. The Time Cards are stored, alphabetically, by enrollee name, in a kit which should be kept readily available to enrollees, but placed near the coordinator.

d. Each time an enrollee begins a new programmed book, a new Time Card must be used. All Time Cards covering completed programmed books are placed in the enrollee's permanent file, after notation is made by the coordinator on the appropriate Progression Chart.

Coordinator Performance
Check List

CHAPTER FIVE

COORDINATOR PERFORMANCE CHECK LIST

Have I:

1. become familiar with the learning lab concept?

2. familiarized myself with the objectives of the learning lab and the educational program in which I am working?

3. provided the learning lab with adequate physical facilities?

4. organized the materials in ascending order of difficulty by subject?

5. taken the placement inventories and analyzed my results for placement in a program?

6. studied in detail the content of each programmed text, teacher's manual and test booklet?

7. read at least one text on the theory and use of programmed instruction?

8. practiced the testing, counseling and placement with a person with whom I am familiar—other than a student?

9. placed the student "on step" within the curriculum?

10. developed my role as a facilitator or tutor in the learning process rather than as a giver of information (teacher)?

11. caused the student to state verbally his objectives?

12. asked the student to perform at his own level of comprehension?

Do I understand:

1. the curriculum guides and placement charts?

2. the procedures and methodology of the learning lab?

3. the various counseling techniques used by the coordinator?

4. the biographical data form and how to collect the important information?

5. tests and inventories and the characteristics of each?

6. principles of learning and how they can be implemented in the learning lab?

7. the sequence and continuity of the learning lab system and how this is used in tailoring a curriculum for each student?

8. how to establish a realistic schedule for each student?

Do I:

1. believe that the learning lab approach to instruction is a valid one?

2. believe in the dignity and worth of each student who comes to the laboratory?

3. have a sincere desire to accept, understand and help each student?

4. know how to establish rapport with each student, open the lines of communication and develop a good working relationship with each student?

5. allow the program to do the teaching and myself to serve as a facilitator or catalyst in the learning process?

6. greet each student with warmth?

7. observe my students for signs of frustration?

8. go over and establish communication when signs of frustration are present?

9. maintain control of the lab and serve as a supervisor?

10. allow and/or encourage in indirect ways my students to become independent?

11. administer periodic tests and make sure each student is achieving at a high rate of comprehension (85 percent)?

Can I:

analyze the results of counseling, testing and objectives and develop a meaningful curriculum for each student?

An Example

APPENDIX A

AN EXAMPLE: LEARNING LABORATORIES FOR ADULTS IN NORTH CAROLINA

North Carolina is one of the most populous essentially rural states in the nation. Yet industrialization and urbanization are running rampant in North Carolina. The state's rural populace is migrating to urban areas within the state and to other more urban states. A majority of these migrants are in need of instruction to improve literacy and vocational, industrial, technical and, in many instances, social skills.

In 1963, our educational and political leaders recognized the need for an educational program that would meet the needs of every adult who is unemployed, underemployed and/or desirous of more educational training. In the same year, the North Carolina General Assembly established the Department of Community Colleges.

During the past several years, 30 technical institutes and 20 community colleges have been established and are now operational. It has become possible to extend universal educational opportunity to every adult, regardless of his previous educational experience.

In accordance with an "open door" policy, any person who is 18 years of age or older and who desires more education can find the opportunity for further education— consonant with his abilities, needs, and interests. The student is admitted regardless of his previous educational background and his present measured ability. He is tested and counseled, not in order to reject him if he does not meet a set educational standard, but to help him be placed properly.

The imposed "open door" policy caused community college personnel to think seriously about various curricula and practical teaching methods that would cover the entire range of subjects. One basic problem was, How could one institution offer all subjects to such a heterogeneous group of students? After months of research and planning, the learning laboratory was developed as an aid in the implementation of the policy of the open door.

The first learning laboratory was installed in January, 1964. The success of the first facility initiated an expansion. To date, 60 comprehensive labs are in operation, plus 20 "Mini-Labs." The comprehensive labs include subjects from grade levels 1-14, and Mini-Labs are designed especially for use in Adult Basic Education and include grades 1-8.

Since the inception of the learning labs in the community college, the learning lab concept has spread into adult education (Adult Learning centers), Neighborhood Youth centers, Job Corps centers, public schools, prison and correctional centers, colleges and universities. Some ten additional states have implemented similar programs.

OBJECTIVES

With programs for any level of comprehension, the laboratories are basically designed for the following goals: (1) to give basic instruction in literacy training for grades 1-8, (2) to enable one to prepare for the General Educational Development Examination (a GED curriculum has been constructed), (3) to allow one to prepare for specific examinations (Federal Service Entrance Examination and Adult High School Diploma battery in North Carolina),

(4) to correct weak subject areas by giving basic instruction or review work, (5) to offer pre-college work in a variety of subjects such as reading, vocabulary, mathematics, foreign language, physics and chemistry, (6) to help a student keep pace in a selected trade, technical, industrial, vocational or college parallel curriculum, and (7) to permit one to better himself through academic and selected courses of general interest.

The validity of the General Educational Development Curriculum was tested using students who entered with an average reading level of eighth grade. During a period of 12-18 months, six hundred students completed their individual curriculum. Of these, 588 (or 98 percent) passed all sub-tests.

BASIC MATERIALS

The initial materials supplied to the majority of labs include 17 programs and kits in reading, 16 in English and language arts, 19 in arithmetic, 13 in mathematics, 9 in social studies, 8 in science, 5 in business, 5 in foreign language, and a variety of additional programs including such subjects as psychology, statistics, slide rule, physics, medical terminology, basic patient care, mathematics for nursing, air conditioning, applied electricity, sheet metal layout, basic electronics, interview tapes, vocabulary improvement, phonetics, calculus and trigonometry for physical science.

Forty-nine of the above provide instruction typically given to students prior to the ninth grade, 32 programs teach high school subjects and skills, and the additional unclassified programs teach vocational-technical skills or appeal to adult interests.

ENROLLMENT AND COST

During the spring quarter of 1968, there were 5,692 students actively enrolled in the 60 comprehensive labs. Three thousand three hundred twenty-seven or 58 percent were below eighth grade; 2,870 or 50 percent were male; 2,240 or 39 percent were non-white; 3,327 or 58 percent were enrolled in high school preparation; 1,231 or 21.6 percent in academic; 840 or 14.7 percent in vocational-trade; and 294 or 5 percent in general interest. The average entering level was seventh grade.

The total cost of a comprehensive lab will vary from $4,000 to $6,000, excluding equipment and physical facilities. Once the purpose or educational objective is known, material can be compiled to achieve the goal—which will determine the cost. The number of students that can be accommodated with the initial allocation of materials is almost unlimited and in most cases can be controlled by the space available.

ACCOMPLISHMENTS

A few of the accomplishments of the learning labs concept thus far are:

1. It has advanced nonreaders to literacy level and a few to high school graduation equivalency. This required initial and comprehensive instruction in reading, English, math, science and social studies.

2. It has provided the basic academic skills necessary for admittance into the curriculum and mastery of vocational level training—auto mechanics, bricklaying and many other trades. This required both initial and remedial instruction through literacy level. Many students have made the transition.

3. It has provided the advanced academic skills and knowledge necessary for admittance into the mastery of technical and college level instruction—electronics, computer programming and other two-year post high school degree programs, and in both liberal arts and technical college

programs. Several hundred students have progressed into technical work and many have enrolled in college.

4. It has provided immediate remedial instruction.

5. Many institutions are admitting students into curricula pending the removal of deficiencies by assigned work in the lab.

6. In many locations, students are assigned to the learning laboratory as a preliminary to classroom activity in science and related courses.

EXPANSION OF THE LEARNING LABORATORY

When the first learning laboratory opened its doors to students in Asheboro in January of 1964, North Carolina scored a "first"—the advent of wide-spread use of programmed materials to instruct students outside of the structure of a traditional classroom.

The future use of programmed instruction in North Carolina and elsewhere is not limited, however, to the learning laboratory itself. Within the public school system, the labs could become the axis around which an entire learning resource center would develop, serving both the schools and the community at large. One such center has already been established in North Carolina.

In addition, such instructional materials could considerably lighten the load of the teacher, providing him with increased time to devote to students who are in need of individualized attention.

The classroom would, in short, move toward a subtype of the ungraded classroom in which slow learners in one or more areas of study could be given remedial work to bring them up to the average achievement for their assigned grade level while the gifted students would be able to surge forward at their own speed into previously uncharted areas. In this way, the teacher could better meet the needs of slow, average and fast learners while the students themselves would be challenged at the levels at which they could achieve success.

Programmed materials can provide business and industry with more qualified personnel, persons who are at a level at which they can effectively carry out the responsibilities of highly skilled jobs. In addition, the use of programmed instruction simplifies the process of on-the-job or in-service training.

This case study of learning lab use (in this instance, with an adult student population) is reprinted from *Educational Technology* Magazine, © 1968 Educational Technology Publications.

Program Evaluation

APPENDIX B

PROGRAM EVALUATION

The evaluation of a learning laboratory begins at its formation and continues throughout its implementation and development. The success or failure of the lab is very much dependent on the use of objectives. As the purpose of evaluation is to determine the extent to which objectives are actually being accomplished, it is necessary that the evaluation procedures give feedback about each level of objectives. These objectives can be defined and ordered in terms of the administrator of the learning laboratory, the objectives of the coordinator, and the objectives of the learner. Objectives are stated and evaluated in relation to the behavioral change sought, the content area in which the behavioral change is to take place, and the value placed on the changed behavior.

Throughout the laboratory development process, evaluation is imperative for replanning, redevelopment and reappraisal on every level. Follow-up studies from the information gathered from the performance of the student and the content of the programmed instruction should also be instituted. The criteria for the acceptance of programs will help determine not only the effectiveness of the lab, but the quality of the programs which will be made available in years to come.

The assessment of the student in the laboratory begins the moment the prospective student and the coordinator meet for the first time, and continues until the goals of the student have been reached. Evaluation through testing and observation of the student's behavior is necessary to determine the impact of the learning program on the student; and it is, of course, only through this procedure that one can reach conclusions about the effectiveness of the learning laboratory.

Methods of Evaluating
Programmed Instruction Materials

APPENDIX C

METHODS OF EVALUATING
PROGRAMMED INSTRUCTION MATERIALS

In using programmed instruction, the burden of instructional effectiveness is on the program. This being the case, the selection of materials becomes a more vital decision than it is in choosing conventional textbooks. This makes it imperative that the person who is responsible for choosing materials have a reliable method of evaluating the many different programs that will be available to him.

Publishers of programs for the past several years have been exhorted to include a validation statement with their programs. Such a statement, if included, provides a summary of the conditions that were met in the research, development, and testing of the program. If a validation statement is not included, and if one cannot be obtained upon request by the potential user, then it is difficult to make any accurate assessment of whether or not the program can actually do what it is purportedly designed to do, except through long-term, "on-site" testing, which is impractical for most users.

Criteria which, if included in the validation statement, provide adequate information with which to judge the program are:

- *Learner Population*: A general description of how the subjects were selected, their entering levels in terms of age, educational level, and I.Q. should be contained as prerequisite knowledge for any program.
- *Assessment*: The program should include a pretest-posttest design based upon the stipulated behavioral objectives of the program. All test items must be related to objectives and the reliability of all instruments included.
- *Objectives*: The objectives of the program should be clearly stated in terms of what the learner should be able to do upon completion of the unit.

These should be defined in unambiguous terms, delineating conditions of performance and levels of proficiency to be obtained.

- *Conditions of field testing*: Conditions under which the experimental population were exposed should be stated as well as the number in the group at the beginning and completion of the testing. Other parameters included should be the location of the testing area, the time requirements for completing the program, achievement levels, and motivation given by the tester.
- *Recommendations for use*: The programmed text should give some suggestions for program administration as indicated by the producer's experience and include a teacher's and a student's manual. Within the teacher's manual, there should be an interpretation and scoring key for all test items. The student's manual should contain a statement which informs the learner why it is important to learn the particular unit.

Although the specifics within validation statements vary with the program, the foregoing are deemed essential, to assist a coordinator in the task of selecting effective programs with an educated judgment.

Auto-Instructional Machines System

APPENDIX D

AUTO-INSTRUCTIONAL MACHINES SYSTEM

Listed below is a partial list of recommended auto-tutorial equipment:

Tape Recorder—A machine with a reel or cassette for prepared tapes or developing applicable programs designed for earphone use.

Record Player—A machine for playing records designed for earphone use.

Filmstrip Projector with Cassette Recorder and Record Player—An individual audiovisual machine with prepared filmstrips with corresponding prepared tapes or records and a small screen for viewing. Earphones may be used.

Tachistoscope—An individual reading machine for pacing or accelerating reading, for developing eye muscle control and proper visual coordination in reading.

Controlled Reader—An instrument with viewing area which contains both tachistoscope and pacer features.

Pacer—An individual manual or electric machine with screen developed to encourage or increase the reading pace.

General Teaching Machines—Individual manual or electrical instruments designed to teach programmed material and reinforce learning in a variety of subject areas.

Overhead Projector—A machine designed to visually present on transparencies information for orientation programs and subject matter areas.

8mm Single Concept Projector—A film projector for individual use, which utilizes a removable cartridge-type film for continuous rerun.

Independent Study Film Projector—A small individual movie projector.

Dial Access Retrieval System—A sound system having storage and retrieval capabilities from reel to reel or cassette programs. These programs can be dialed into by students from various local stations with either monitor response, self-recording, playback, or tutorial features.

Vendors

APPENDIX E

VENDORS

This is the era of change, a time in which automation and technology have begun to reform education. Technology is greatly influencing educational methods and objectives. It provides the development of equipment and materials which are desperately needed in the individualized learning program.

The majority of materials are supplied by the following vendors:

Addison-Wesley Publishing
Company, Inc.
Reading, Massachusetts 01867

Allyn and Bacon, Inc.
470 Atlantic Avenue
Boston, Massachusetts 02210

Appleton-Century-Crofts
440 Park Avenue South
New York, New York 10016

Argyle Publishing Corporation
200 Madison Avenue
New York, New York 10016

Behavioral Research
Laboratories
Box 577
Palo Alto, California

R.R. Bowker Company
1180 Avenue of the Americas
New York, New York 10036

California Test Bureau
Division of McGraw-Hill
Book Company
Del Monte Research Park
Monterey, California 93940

Central Scientific Company
1700 Irving Park Road
Chicago, Illinois 60611

Coronet Learning Programs
Coronet Instructional Films
65 East S. Water Street
Chicago, Illinois 60601

Doubleday & Company, Inc.
501 Franklin Avenue
Garden City, New York 10017

Dupont Industrial
Training Service
Room 7450
Nemours Building
Wilmington, Delaware 19898

Education Engineering, Inc.
381 W. Seventh Street
San Pedro, California 90731

Educational Services and
Supplies Co., Inc.
261 Alhambra Circle
Coral Gables, Florida 33134

Educational Systems Development
31270 Stephenson Hwy.
P.O. Box 457
Royal Oak, Michigan 48068

The Effective Learning Corp.
28 West Canal Street
Navaree, Ohio 44662

Encyclopaedia Brittanica Press
425 N. Michigan Avenue
Chicago, Illinois 60611

Entelek Incorporated
42 Pleasant Street
Newburyport, Massachusetts 01950

Follett Publishing Company
1010 W. Washington Boulevard
Chicago, Illinois 60607

General Learning Corp.
Career Advancement Programs
3 E. 54th Street
New York, New York 10022

Ginn and Company
Statler Building
Boston, Massachusetts 02117

Globe Book Company, Inc.
175 Fifth Avenue
New York, New York 10010

Graflex Education & Training
235 Park Avenue S.
Suite 1200
New York, New York 10003

Grolier Education Corporation
(Teaching Materials Corp.)

575 Lexington Avenue
New York, New York 10022

Harcourt Brace Jovanovich, Inc.
757 Third Avenue
New York, New York 10017

Harper & Row, Publishers, Inc.
49 E. 33rd Street
New York, New York 10016

Hobart Welding School
Trade Square East
Troy, Ohio 45373

Hope College
Holland,
Michigan 49423

Imperial Productions, Inc.
Department K
Kankakee, Illinois 60901

Instructional Materials
Availability Center

Office of Instructional Resources
University of Illinois at
Chicago Circle
Box 4348
Chicago, Illinois 60680

International Educational
Services, Inc.
Division of International
Textbook Company
Department 852A
Scranton, Pennsylvania 18515

Lyons & Carnahan, Inc.
407 E. 25th Street
Chicago, Illinois 60616

The Macmillan Company
866 Third Avenue
New York, New York 10022

McCormic-Mathers Publishing
Company, Inc.
Wichita, Kansas 67201

McGraw-Hill Book Company
330 W. 42nd Street
New York, New York 10036

Medical College of
Georgia Bookstore
Augusta, Georgia 30902

Charles E. Merrill Books, Inc.
1300 Alum Creek Drive
Columbus, Ohio 43216

National Education Association
1201 16th Street, N.W.
Washington, D.C. 20036

Noble & Noble Publishers, Inc.
750 Third Avenue
New York, New York 10017

Prentice-Hall, Inc.
Englewood Cliffs,
New Jersey 07632

The Psychological Corp.
304 East 45th Street
New York, New York 10017

J. Ravin Publications
P.O. Box 114
El Segundo, California 90245

Resources Development Corp.
P.O. Box 591
East Lansing, Michigan 48823

Frank E. Richards
Publishing Company, Inc.
215 Church Street
Phoenix, New York 13135

W.B. Saunders Company
W. Washington Square
Philadelphia, Pennsylvania 19105

Science Research Associates, Inc.
259 E. Erie Street
Chicago, Illinois 60611

Society for Visual
Education, Inc.
1345 Diversey Parkway
Chicago, Illinois 60614

University of Chicago Press
Chicago,
Illinois 60637

Vimcet Associates
P.O. Box 24714
Los Angeles, California 90024

Vocab Incorporated
3071 South Broad Street
Chicago, Illinois 60608

John Wiley & Sons, Inc.
605 Third Avenue
New York, New York 10016

Xerox Corporation
600 Madison Avenue
New York, New York 10022

Notes